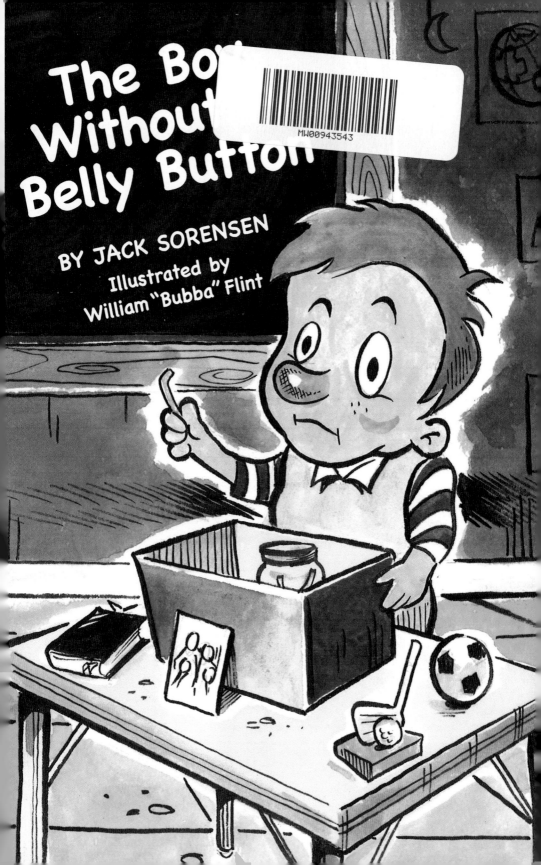

The Boy Without a Belly Button

BY JACK SORENSEN

Illustrated by
William "Bubba" Flint

ISBN: 1499508824
ISBN 13:9781499508826
Library of Congress Control Number: 2014908770
CreateSpace Independent Publishing Platform
North Charleston, South Carolina

THE BOY WITHOUT A BELLY BUTTON

It was the first day of school, and I was excited to get back to all my friends. I was sick of my stinky little brother and listening to my mom telling me what to do all summer.

Mrs. Babilla walked into class and welcomed all the students.

"On Friday", Mrs. Babilla said, "everyone is to bring a "Me Box".

"A Me Box"? the class questioned.

"Let me explain", and she held up a small colorful box as she continued. "This small box will contain items that represent you and your life. Meaning things you enjoy, people you love, and anything unique about you".

Reed asked, "How can I fit my dog in there?" The class laughed hysterically. Julie giggled and shouted out, " What about my little sister?" "and how about my swimming pool" shouted out Will.

"Class, calm down! calm down!", Mrs. Babilla yelled in the teacher tone all teachers have, not too loud but loud enough to know we need to stop and pay attention. "The items must fit in this box, so place pictures, small items, anything that will fit, and nothing alive"! She smiled a warm smiled.

"How was your first day"? mom asked me before I could put my books down.

"It was easy, but we got an assignment the first day of school", I said with disappointment

"Really, mom said, "as she emptied the dishwasher".

"Yeah, it's a box I have to fill up with stuff about me, unique stuff. You know like my golf trophies, and my soccer shoes. You know...stuff."

"Oh, cool. why don't you get on it now so we don't have to do it last minute".

That's what she always says about homework.

Get on it now so you don't have to worry about it later. She says she is training me for middle school!

I worked all week on my box. I added my golf trophy, where I came in third place. I was really proud. I added a small soccer ball to represent my love for sports, a picture of my family and my Bible. I needed one more thing to really make it me...

Thursday night as I was completing my Me Box, I was really thinking hard about something unique. "Mom, should I put in my staples"?

Mom stood speechless. "You think so? I think it would be a great idea," she said. She smiled at me and I think she had a tear in her eye. Why do moms do that?

"I am scared, but I think I am ready". She gave me a look of reassurance and smiled, and said "I have no doubt you can do it, you can do anything".

Friday morning, the Me Box presentations begin. First up was Gail.

"My name is Gail and I have a beautiful Barbie, and cheerleading pom poms because I love cheerleading! And a picture of my grandmother, because she is my favorite relative. She always gives me candy".

Then we have our class clown, Reed. "Hi, I am Reed, I couldn't bring my dog so here is his picture. I have a picture of my family because my mom made me, then there is a bag of chips that I love and a Slurpee cup, my favorite treat"!

Third up is me, Jack. I stand up, I am nervous. I start by saying "Hi my name is Jack, my me box contains stuff about me. Like this golf trophy that I won. I came in third place, and that was cool." I held up a picture next. "This is my family because I love them. I have two sides because my parents are divorced, but I love them both. This is a small soccer ball. I love sports, anything with a ball". And then something unique...."

My stomach is in a knot, I am beet red, and I feel like I could pass out... Then I hold up a jar of staples and I say it.

"I don't have a Belly Button!"

The class gasps and then Reed asks "Are you an alien?"

WOW! I said it, and now everyone knows my little secret.

"These staples were used on me the day I was born. I was born with an omphalocele. That means all my organs were outside my body when I was in my mom."

My feelings were hurt at first only because the class didn't understand, and I had never talked about it before. The girls thought it was cool, and I guess it kinda is. After the shock of it all, it was no big deal. I was just like everyone else.

Then it was time for the next me box presentation, no one was going to have a unique thing like me. Nobody!

That weekend, I went to a swim party. I always have worn a swim-shirt. I have always hidden my scar from everyone. I thought now, since everyone knows about my scar, I don't have to hide it. It was the first time I didn't wear a swim-shirt. I felt good about myself, it was more comfortable. I did prefer being underwater for the first half, but then I was really ok walking around and just being me.

I can do anything anyone else can do. You don't really need a bellybutton to do stuff. However, one thing that is hard with no bellybutton, is sports. With an omphalocele, you might not be able to play contact sports, like football and hockey. When the doctors place your organs back into your body, everything might not fall back in place where they are suppose to go. In my case, my liver is lower than it should be and not protected by my rib cage. So no football for me. But soccer, basketball, baseball everything else, I am the best!

You have to always watch out for people hitting you in the stomach, because you are very tender there and it hurts extra hard when you get hit.

Even though I have had my scar all of my life, I still sometimes have a hard time telling people about it. But it's ok, because people will think its really cool when your older. And it doesn't matter if you have one or not you just need to have fun.

If someone makes fun of you, tell them to stop, then tell your parents.

If you are ever sad about not having a belly button, be glad your alive.

I am glad to be alive. My mom says I am a miracle.